Power Whispers

Speak the Word. Renew the Mind.

Eugene S. Fritz

Copyright

 All scripture quotations are adapted or paraphrased for clarity unless otherwise noted.

Table of Contents

Chapter 1

The Power of Speaking the Word

Most people read the Bible silently. They open a page, scan the words with their eyes, think about what they mean, and then move on with their day. Reading scripture is good. It nourishes the mind and teaches the heart. But the Bible repeatedly points to something more powerful than simply reading. It points to **speaking**.

Again and again, scripture emphasizes the power of words spoken aloud — words heard by the ears and carried into the heart.

One of the clearest statements appears in **Epistle to the Romans 10:17**:

"Faith comes by hearing, and hearing by the word of God."

Notice something important. The verse does not say faith comes by reading.

It says faith comes by **hearing**.

Hearing activates something deeper. When we hear truth repeatedly, it begins to shape how we think, what we believe, and how we respond to life.

And whose voice do we hear most often?

Our own.

When we speak scripture aloud, we are not simply reading words from a page. We are allowing our own ears to hear the truth of God's Word. That truth begins to replace fear, doubt, and uncertainty with faith.

This is why the Bible repeatedly connects **the Word and the mouth**.

In **Epistle to the Romans 10:8**, Paul writes:

"The word is near you; it is in your mouth and in your heart."

The Word was never meant to live only on a page. It was meant to live in **the mouth and the heart** of the believer.

Speaking the Word brings it from the page into daily life.

Words Shape the Direction of Life

The Bible takes spoken words very seriously.

In **Book of Proverbs 18:21**, we are told:

"Death and life are in the power of the tongue."

Few statements in scripture are as direct as this one.

Our words carry power. They influence the direction of our thinking, the atmosphere around us, and the beliefs we carry inside.

Many people unintentionally speak defeat over themselves every day.

"I'll never get out of this situation."

"Nothing ever works for me."

"I'm not strong enough."

Over time, words like these shape the way we see the world.

But scripture offers another way.

Instead of repeating fear, we can **speak truth**.

Instead of declaring defeat, we can declare what God says.

This is the heart of the Power Whisper practice.

Faith Speaks

Faith in the Bible is not silent.

In **Second Epistle to the Corinthians 4:13**, Paul writes:

"I believed, therefore I have spoken."

Belief and speech are connected. When faith is alive inside a person, it eventually comes out through the mouth.

We see this principle throughout the Bible.

When God instructed Joshua how to live successfully, He said something very specific in **Book of Joshua 1:8**:

"This Book of the Law shall not depart from your mouth, but you shall meditate on it day and night."

Notice the instruction.

The Word should not depart from **the mouth**.

Meditation in the ancient biblical sense often involved softly repeating scripture. Repetition rewires the mind. People would quietly speak the words again and again,

allowing them to sink deeply into the heart. **Joshua 1:8,** meditating on it day and night.
This practice turns scripture into something living rather than something merely read.

This practice turns scripture into something living rather than something merely read.

Jesus Modeled This Practice

Jesus Himself demonstrated the power of spoken scripture.

When He faced temptation in the wilderness, He did not argue or debate. Instead, He responded with a simple phrase:

"It is written."

Each time the temptation came, Jesus answered with scripture spoken aloud.

This pattern appears in **Gospel of Matthew 4:4**, 4:7, and 4:10.

Every challenge was met with the same strategy:

Speak the Word.

Jesus showed that truth spoken aloud carries authority.

Words Direct the Course of Life

The New Testament book of James gives another powerful picture of the importance of speech.

In **Epistle of James 3:5**, we read:

"The tongue is a small part of the body, but it makes great boasts."

James compares the tongue to the rudder of a ship.

A rudder is small compared to the size of a ship, yet it determines the direction the entire vessel travels.

Our words function in a similar way.

The things we repeatedly say begin to guide the direction of our lives.

Because of this, scripture encourages us to guard our speech.

In **Epistle to the Ephesians 4:29**, we are told:

"Let no corrupt communication proceed out of your mouth, but only what is helpful for building others up."

Words should give life, not tear down.

Speaking God's Word Releases Power

The Bible also teaches that God's Word carries power when it is spoken.

In **Book of Isaiah 55:11**, God declares:

"My word... shall not return to me empty but will accomplish what I desire."

God's Word is not merely information. It is living and active.

When we speak scripture, we are aligning our words with God's truth.

We are allowing His Word to shape our thinking and strengthen our faith.

Over time, something remarkable happens.

Fear begins to lose its voice.

Doubt grows quieter.

Faith becomes stronger.

From Reading to Speaking

Reading scripture feeds the mind.

Speaking scripture feeds the heart.

When the Word moves from the page to the mouth, and from the mouth to the ears, it begins to settle deeper within us.

This is why the Power Whisper practice focuses on **short scriptures spoken slowly and intentionally**.

Not shouted.

Not rushed.

Simply spoken.

Soft enough to hear.

Clear enough to believe.

Each whisper becomes a seed planted in the heart.

And as scripture promises, what is planted will eventually grow.

In the next section, we will explore how to turn these truths into a simple daily practice called **Power Whispers**—a five-minute routine that helps strengthen faith, renew the mind, and align our words with God's promises.

Side note: The **Science Behind Speaking**

Why Speaking Changes Memory

You may wonder why speaking scripture aloud matters more than reading it silently.

There is science behind this.

Researchers call it the **"production effect."**

Studies show that words we produce ourselves—by speaking them aloud—are remembered significantly better than words we simply read or hear.

When you speak a word, your brain engages multiple systems at once:

- **Motor planning** (forming the sounds)
- **Auditory processing** (hearing what you say)
- **Memory encoding** (storing the experience)

This multi-sensory engagement creates a stronger memory trace than reading alone.

Research in cognitive psychology, often called the 'production effect,' shows that people tend to remember words better when they speak them aloud rather than read them silently

This isn't just about faith.

It's about how the human brain works.

When you whisper scripture, you're not just repeating words.

You're creating a deeper imprint in your mind.

And that imprint lasts longer.

Why This Matters for Power Whispers

This is why the Power Whisper practice emphasizes **speaking slowly and hearing clearly**.

You're not just going through motions.

You're using your brain's natural design to help truth stick.

The ancient practice of speaking scripture aligns with modern understanding of memory and learning.

Faith and science, in this case, point in the same direction.

A Note on the Research

The production effect has been studied across multiple contexts:

- Language learning
- Memory retention
- Educational psychology

The findings are consistent: **speaking improves recall.**

This doesn't diminish the spiritual dimension of the practice.

It simply confirms that the method works the way it was designed to.

Chapter 2

The Power Whisper Method ™

Your mind is always listening. Make sure it is listening to truth.

The idea behind Power Whispers is simple.

You speak the Word of God quietly enough to hear it clearly.

Not as a performance.
Not as a long prayer.
Not as something complicated.

Just a few words of truth spoken slowly.

The goal is not volume. The goal is **hearing**.

When scripture is spoken aloud, your ears hear the Word, your mind processes it, and your heart begins to believe it. Over time, the truth of scripture becomes stronger than the negative thoughts, fears, and doubts that often fill our minds.

A Power Whisper is simply **scripture spoken quietly and intentionally**.

Why Whisper?

Whispering slows us down.

When people speak loudly or quickly, they often rush through words without truly hearing them. But whispering forces us to move slowly and deliberately.

Each word becomes clear.

Each phrase becomes meaningful.

A whisper also creates focus. It quiets the noise around us and helps us concentrate on what we are saying.

The point is not to impress anyone.

The point is to **hear the Word**.

The Five-Minute Practice

The Power Whisper practice takes only a few minutes each day.

Five minutes is enough.

You do not need a long routine. Consistency is far more powerful than length.

A simple routine might look like this:

Step 1 — Sit Quietly

Sit somewhere comfortable. This could be in a chair, at the edge of your bed, or anywhere you can take a few quiet moments.

Take a slow breath and allow your mind to settle.

Place one hand on your belly
and one hand on your heart.

Breathe in slowly through your nose for the count of 4.
Feel your breath fill your belly.

Breathe out slowly for the count of 4.
Feel your heart relax.

Another option is humming. Hum for one or two minutes before going to next step.

Step 2 — Speak the Scripture

Choose a short verse and whisper it slowly.

For example:

"The Lord is my light and my salvation. I will not fear."
Book of Psalms 27:1

Speak the words softly.

Hear every word.

Step 3 — Repeat the Whisper

Say the verse again.

Let the meaning sink in.

The goal is not repetition for the sake of repetition. The goal is to allow the truth to settle deeper in your heart each time you speak it.

Step 4 — Speak Two or Three Verses

After repeating the first whisper a few times, move to another verse.

For example:

"God has not given me a spirit of fear, but of power, love, and a sound mind."
Second Epistle to Timothy 1:7

Then another:

"With God nothing shall be impossible."
Gospel of Luke 1:37

Three verses are enough.

A Simple Example Routine

Morning Power Whisper:

1. "Thank you that I am blessed with all spiritual blessings in Christ."
   Ephesians 1:3
2. "Thank you that the peace of God guards my heart and mind."
   Philippians 4:7
3. "I can do all things through Christ who strengthens me."
   Epistle to the Philippians 4:13

Whisper each verse two or three times.

The entire practice takes about five minutes.

What you repeat rewires your mind.

Consistency Is the Key

One day of Power Whispers is helpful.

But the real strength comes from repeating the practice daily.

Just as seeds grow slowly beneath the soil, the Word grows quietly within the heart when it is spoken and heard regularly.

You may not notice change immediately.

But over time, something begins to shift.

Fear becomes quieter.

Faith becomes stronger.

Peace becomes more natural.

And the words you speak begin to shape the way you see the world.

The Purpose of Power Whispers

Power Whispers are not about trying to control life with words.

They are about aligning our words with **God's truth**.

When we speak scripture, we are reminding ourselves of what God has already said.

We are allowing His Word to guide our thoughts, strengthen our faith, and shape our actions.

In the next section, we will begin exploring specific Power Whispers from scripture, short verses organized by themes such as faith, courage, provision, peace, relationships, and purpose.

These whispers are simple, powerful, and designed to be spoken daily.

When you speak, you are not just thinking, you are guiding your mind.

What to Do When It Feels Silly

There will be a moment.

Maybe it's the third day. Maybe it's the seventh. You'll be sitting quietly, ready to whisper the Word, and a voice will rise up inside you.

"This feels strange."

"Is anyone else doing this?"

"Do I really need to say this out loud?"

"What if someone walks in and hears me?"

This voice is not unusual.

It is human.

Almost everyone who begins the Power Whisper practice experiences this resistance. It is not a sign that the practice is wrong. It is a sign that you are stepping outside your comfort zone.

The Awkward Week

The first week of any new habit often feels awkward.

Your brain is wired for familiarity. When you introduce something new, especially something that involves speaking quietly to yourself, it triggers a natural hesitation.

This is normal.

Think of it like learning to play an instrument. The first time you hold a guitar, your fingers feel clumsy. The strings don't respond the way you expect. You wonder if you're doing it right.

But with time, the fingers learn. The strings respond. The music flows.

The same is true with Power Whispers.

The first few days may feel unnatural. You may feel self-conscious. You may question whether this is truly helping.

Give yourself permission to feel this way.

Do not judge yourself for it.

Simply continue.

A Story of Persistence
There is a story told about Anthony the Great, a monk who lived in the Egyptian desert.

He devoted his life to prayer and solitude. Yet even he faced moments of doubt.

One evening, sitting alone in his cell, he felt a deep sense of foolishness.
He was speaking words of faith into an empty room.
No one was there to hear him. No one to affirm him.

He wondered if he was wasting his time.

Then he remembered something he had been taught:
The value of prayer is not found in how it feels, but in the truth of what is spoken.

So he continued.

Day after day.

Week after week.

Years later, when others asked him about his faith, he would say:

"I learned to trust the Word more than my feelings."

You may not be in a desert cell.

But you may feel the same way.

Alone.

Unsure.

Wondering if anyone is listening.

The answer is yes.

The Inner Critic

That voice inside you—the one that says this is silly—is what psychologists call the "inner critic."

It is not your enemy.

It is a protective mechanism.

Your mind is trying to keep you safe from embarrassment, from failure, from standing out.

But faith often requires standing out.

Faith often requires doing something that feels vulnerable.

When you whisper scripture, you are choosing truth over comfort.

You are choosing belief over doubt.

You are choosing to speak life even when your feelings say otherwise.

Practical Strategies

If you find yourself resisting the practice, try these approaches:

1. Start Small

If five minutes feels too long, start with two.

If speaking feels too exposed, whisper so quietly only you can hear.

The goal is consistency, not perfection.

2. Change Your Location

If you feel self-conscious in your usual spot, try a different place.

A closet.

A car.

A park bench.

A quiet corner of your bedroom.

Wherever you feel safe.

3. Remember the Purpose

You are not performing.

You are not trying to impress anyone.

You are aligning your heart with truth.

The audience is not other people.

The audience is your own soul.

4. Track Your Progress

Keep a simple mark on a calendar for each day you complete the practice.

Seeing the streak grow can motivate you to continue.

5. Be Kind to Yourself

If you miss a day, do not restart.

Do not punish yourself.

Simply begin again the next day.

Grace is part of the practice.

The Turning Point

There will come a day when the awkwardness fades.

You will sit down to whisper the Word and feel a sense of calm instead of resistance.

You will hear the scripture and feel it settle deeper than before.

You will realize that the voice that once said *"this is silly"* has grown quieter.

And the voice of faith has grown louder.

This is the turning point.

It usually happens around the second or third week.

Until then, trust the process.

Trust the Word.

Trust yourself.

A Final Thought

The greatest saints of history were not those who never felt doubt.

They were those who spoke truth anyway.

They whispered faith when they felt fear.

They declared hope when they felt despair.

They trusted God when they felt alone.

You are walking the same path.

And you are not alone.

Next Section

Now that you understand the resistance you may face, you are ready to move forward.

In the next section, we will explore the specific Power Whispers themselves, short scriptures organized by theme, ready for you to speak and hear.

Choose your first whisper.

Speak it slowly.

And remember:

Even when it feels silly, it is still sacred.

Chapter 3

The Power Whispers

Power Whispers are short scriptures spoken slowly and intentionally.

Each whisper comes directly from the Bible and is written so it can be spoken personally. When spoken softly and consistently, these words help anchor the heart in truth and strengthen faith.

You do not need to speak every whisper each day. Choose **two or three**, whisper them slowly, and allow the words to settle into your heart.

Over time, these truths begin to shape your thoughts, your speech, and the way you walk through life.

Faith

Power Whisper

The Lord is my light and my salvation; I will not fear.
Book of Psalms 27:1

Power Whisper

I walk by faith and not by sight.
Second Epistle to the Corinthians 5:7

Power Whisper

With God nothing is impossible for me.
Gospel of Luke 1:37

Power Whisper

I trust in the Lord with all my heart.
Book of Proverbs 3:5

Power Whisper

The Lord strengthens my heart.
Book of Psalms 31:24

Courage and Mental Strength

Power Whisper

God has not given me a spirit of fear, but power, love, and a sound mind.
Second Epistle to Timothy 1:7

Power Whisper

The Lord is with me wherever I go.
Book of Joshua 1:9

Power Whisper

The Lord is my helper; I will not be afraid.
Epistle to the Hebrews 13:6

Power Whisper

I am strong and courageous.
Book of Joshua 1:9

Power Whisper

The peace of God guards my heart and mind.
Epistle to the Philippians 4:7

Power Whisper

I can do all things through Christ who strengthens me.
Philippians 4:13

Power Whisper

God gave me a strong and peaceful mind.
2 Timothy 1:7

Power Whisper

My mind is renewed by truth.
Romans 12:2

Power Whisper

My mind is strong, clear, and disciplined.
2 Timothy 1:7

Power Whisper

My thoughts align with God's truth.
John 8:32

Identity

Power Whisper

I am fearfully and wonderfully made.
Book of Psalms 139:14

Power Whisper

I am a new creation.
Second Epistle to the Corinthians 5:17

Power Whisper

I am chosen and dearly loved.
Epistle to the Colossians 3:12

Power Whisper

I am God's workmanship.
Epistle to the Ephesians 2:10

Power Whisper

I am a child of God.
Gospel of John 1:12

Power Whisper

God lives in me.
1 Corinthians 3:16

Power Whisper

Christ lives in me.
Galatians 2:20

Power Whisper

God's Spirit lives within me.
1 Corinthians 6:19

Power Whisper

God is working within me.
Philippians 2:13

Power Whisper

I can do all things through Christ who strengthens me.
Philippians 4:13

Success and Purpose

Power Whisper

The Lord directs my steps.
Book of Proverbs 16:9

Power Whisper

I can do all things through Christ who strengthens me.
Epistle to the Philippians 4:13

Power Whisper

The Lord establishes the work of my hands.
Book of Psalms 90:17

Power Whisper

Thank you for giving wisdom liberally to those who ask.
James 1:5

Power Whisper

The Lord guides me continually.
Book of Isaiah 58:11

Power Whisper

The plans God has for me are good.
Book of Jeremiah 29:11

Provision and Finance

Power Whisper

My God supplies all my needs.
Epistle to the Philippians 4:19

Power Whisper

The Lord is my shepherd; I lack nothing.
Book of Psalms 23:1

Power Whisper

The blessing of the Lord brings wealth.
Book of Proverbs 10:22

Power Whisper

God gives me power to create wealth.
Book of Deuteronomy 8:18

Power Whisper

The Lord blesses the work of my hands.
Book of Deuteronomy 28:12

Power Whisper

Thank you for supplying all my needs according to your riches in glory. Philippians 4:19

Health and Life

Power Whisper

I shall live and declare the works of the Lord.
Book of Psalms 118:17

Power Whisper

The Lord restores my soul.
Book of Psalms 23:3

Power Whisper

God heals all my diseases.
Book of Psalms 103:3

Power Whisper

The joy of the Lord is my strength.
Book of Nehemiah 8:10

Power Whisper

"The Lord renews my strength."
Book of Isaiah 40:31

Relationships and Love

Power Whisper

I walk in love toward others.
Epistle to the Ephesians 5:2

Power Whisper

Love is patient and kind in me.
First Epistle to the Corinthians 13:4

Power Whisper

I forgive as the Lord forgave me.
Epistle to the Colossians 3:13

Power Whisper

I am a peacemaker.
Gospel of Matthew 5:9

Power Whisper

I encourage and build others up.
First Epistle to the Thessalonians 5:11

Victory and Protection

Power Whisper

If God is for me, who can be against me?
Epistle to the Romans 8:31

Power Whisper

"I am more than a conqueror
Epistle to the Romans 8:37

Power Whisper

The Lord fights for me.
Book of Exodus 14:14

Power Whisper

No weapon formed against me will prosper.
Book of Isaiah 54:17

Power Whisper

The Lord surrounds me with favor like a shield.
Book of Psalms 5:12

Additional Power Whispers

Power Whisper

The Lord is my refuge and strength.
Book of Psalms 46:1

Power Whisper

The Lord gives wisdom generously.
Epistle of James 1:5

Power Whisper

The Lord goes before me and prepares the way.
Book of Deuteronomy 31:8

Power Whisper

"The Lord is my strength and my shield.
Book of Psalms 28:7

Power Whisper

The Lord fills my heart with peace.
Epistle to the Romans 15:13

Power Whisper

The Lord gives rest to my soul.
Gospel of Matthew 11:28

Power Whisper

The Lord watches over my life.
Book of Psalms 121:7

Power Whisper

The Lord teaches me the way I should go.
Book of Psalms 32:8

Power Whisper

The Lord gives strength to the weary.
Book of Isaiah 40:29

Power Whisper

The Lord fills my life with goodness.
Book of Psalms 23:6

Power Whisper

Thank you that I can do all things through Christ who strengthens me. Philippians 4:13

Power Whisper

Thank you that all things work together for good to those who love you. Romans 8:28

Power Whisper

Thank you that the peace of God guards my heart and mind. Philippians 4:7

Power Whisper

Thank you that I am blessed with all spiritual blessings in Christ. Ephesians 1:3

Power Whisper

Thank you that all things pertaining to life and godliness have been given to me. 2 Peter 1:3

Bonus Power Whispers

Psalm 46:10

I am still. God is in control.

Philippians 4:6–7

I release anxiety. God's peace guards my mind.

Matthew 11:28

I bring my burdens to God. I receive rest.

Isaiah 41:10

I am not alone. God strengthens me.

John 14:27

God's peace is within me. I will not be afraid.

Chapter 4

The Silence That Follows

You have spoken the Word.

You have heard the truth.

Now there is one more step.

Listen.

Why Silence Matters

Speaking is only half of communication.

The other half is listening.

When you finish whispering a scripture, pause.

Sit in silence for thirty seconds.

Let the words settle.

Let the truth land.

This is not empty space.

This is where the Word takes root.

The Biblical Pattern

Throughout scripture, silence plays a vital role.

Elijah stood on the mountain expecting God to speak in wind, earthquake, or fire.

But God did not come in those things.

God came in a **quiet whisper**.

Book of Kings 19:12

"After the earthquake came a fire, but the Lord was not in the fire. And after the fire came a gentle whisper."

Jesus often withdrew to quiet places to pray.

Gospel of Mark 1:35

"Very early in the morning, while it was still dark, Jesus got up, left the house and went off to a solitary place, where he prayed."

Mary sat at Jesus' feet and listened.

Gospel of Luke 10:39

"She had a sister called Mary, who sat at the Lord's feet listening to what he said."

Silence is not absence.

It is presence.

How to Practice Silence

After you finish whispering your three verses:

1. Close Your Eyes

Let the visual world fade.

Turn your attention inward.

2. Breathe Slowly

Take three slow breaths.

Inhale.

Exhale.

3. Wait

Do not rush to the next task.

Do not reach for your phone.

Simply be still.

4. Notice

Pay attention to what arises.

A thought.

A feeling.

A sense of peace.

A memory.

Whatever comes, let it pass.

Return to stillness.

5. Open Gently

When the thirty seconds are complete, open your eyes.

Carry the quiet with you.

What Happens in the Silence

In the silence, something subtle occurs.

The words you spoke begin to integrate.

They move from your mouth to your mind.

From your mind to your heart.

From your heart to your actions.

This integration does not happen instantly.

It happens in the quiet.

Common Challenges

"My mind won't stop racing."

This is normal.

Do not fight the thoughts.

Acknowledge them.

Let them pass.

Return to stillness.

"Thirty seconds feels too long."

Start with ten.

Build gradually.

The capacity grows with practice.

"I feel uncomfortable with silence."

Many people do.

Silence confronts us with ourselves.

But discomfort is not danger.

Stay with it.

The Complete Cycle

The Power Whisper practice is now complete:

Speak → Hear → Listen → Live

1. **Speak** the scripture aloud
2. **Hear** the words with your own ears
3. **Listen** in silence for thirty seconds
4. **Live** the truth throughout your day

This cycle transforms reading into practice.

It transforms information into formation.

A Final Thought

In a world that never stops talking, silence is revolutionary.

It is an act of trust. It is an invitation to receive.

It is a space where faith can grow.

So when you finish your whispers, do not rush away.

Stay in the quiet.

Let the Word settle. Let the truth take root.

And remember:

Sometimes the loudest thing you can do is say nothing at all.

Chapter 5

The 40-Day Power Whisper Challenge

Throughout the Bible, the number **forty** often marks a period of preparation, transformation, and renewal.

Forty days represents a time when something new begins to take shape.

Rain fell for forty days during the great flood before the earth was renewed. Moses spent forty days on Mount Sinai before receiving the commandments. The prophet Elijah traveled forty days through the wilderness before encountering God in a quiet whisper. Even Jesus spent forty days in the wilderness preparing for His ministry.

These seasons of forty days were not random.

They were times of **focus, testing, growth, and spiritual strengthening**.

In the same way, the next forty days are an opportunity to strengthen your faith through the daily practice of speaking God's Word.

Why Forty Days?

Habits grow stronger when practiced consistently.

Speaking scripture each day allows the Word to move from something we occasionally read to something we regularly **hear and believe**.

Over time, these whispers begin to shape how we think, respond, and live.

Forty days gives the practice enough time to become natural.

By the end of the challenge, the habit of speaking truth will likely feel familiar.

How the Challenge Works

The challenge is simple.

Each day, choose **two or three Power Whispers** from the previous section that resonate with you.

Speak them softly.

Repeat each whisper **two or three times**, slowly enough to hear every word.

The entire practice takes about **five minutes**.

Consistency matters far more than length.

A Simple Daily Routine

Morning works best for many people because it sets the tone for the entire day.

Before checking your phone, before the noise of the day begins, take a few quiet moments and whisper the Word.

Example:

Power Whisper 1

"The Lord is my shepherd; I lack nothing."
Book of Psalms 23:1

Power Whisper 2

"God has not given me a spirit of fear."
Second Epistle to Timothy 1:7

Power Whisper 3

"I can do all things through Christ who strengthens me."
Epistle to the Philippians 4:13

Speak each verse slowly.

Hear the truth in your own voice.

What to Expect

During the first few days, the practice may feel new or unfamiliar.

That is normal.

But as the days pass, something begins to shift.

Scripture starts to come to mind more quickly.

Negative thoughts lose their grip more easily.

Faith becomes steadier.

The words you speak begin shaping the atmosphere of your life.

The Goal of the Challenge

This challenge is not about saying the perfect words.

It is about building a habit of **speaking truth daily**.

Each whisper plants a seed.

Some seeds grow quickly.

Others take time.

But as scripture reminds us, seeds planted consistently will eventually produce a harvest.

Begin Today

Choose two or three power whispers.

Speak them slowly.

Hear every word.

Then repeat the practice again tomorrow.

And the next day.

And the next.

Forty days from now, you may be surprised how different your thoughts, your confidence, and your faith feel.

Sometimes transformation begins with something as simple as a whisper.

The Seven Divine Declarations

Words God Instructed People to Speak

Throughout scripture, there are moments when God directs people to **declare something with their mouth**. These spoken words were not random. They affirmed identity, faith, covenant, and trust in God's provision.

These declarations remind us that **spoken words of faith have always been part of the spiritual life**.

1 — The Declaration of Faith

"Hear, O Israel"

Book of Deuteronomy 6:4

"The Lord our God, the Lord is one."

Listen, I am awakening… I am seeking truth… I carry the divine within.

This declaration, known as the **Shema**, was spoken daily by the Israelites. It affirmed their devotion to God and reminded them of who He is.

Divine Declaration

"The Lord our God, the Lord is one."

2 — The Declaration of Gratitude

When Presenting First Fruits

Book of Deuteronomy 26:5

"Then you shall declare before the Lord your God…"

When the Israelites brought offerings, they were instructed to **speak a declaration of gratitude**, remembering how God delivered them.

Divine Declaration

"The Lord has brought me into a land flowing with blessing."

3 — The Declaration of Covenant Identity

Book of Deuteronomy 26:17

"You have declared this day that the Lord is your God."

This declaration affirmed a personal relationship with God.

Divine Declaration

"The Lord is my God, and I will walk in His ways."

4 — The Declaration of God's Faithfulness

Book of Deuteronomy 26:18

"And the Lord has declared this day that you are His people."

This declaration affirmed identity and belonging.

Divine Declaration

"I am God's people, treasured and set apart."

5 — The Declaration of Victory

Book of Psalms 118:17

"I shall not die, but live, and declare the works of the Lord."

This is a bold declaration of life and testimony.

Divine Declaration

"I will live and declare the works of the Lord."

6 — The Declaration of Blessing

Book of Numbers 6:24–26

"Say to them: The Lord bless you and keep you..."

God specifically told the priests to **speak this blessing aloud** over the people.

Divine Declaration

"The Lord blesses me and keeps me.
The Lord makes His face shine upon me and gives me peace."

7 — The Declaration of Salvation

Epistle to the Romans 10:9

"If you declare with your mouth, 'Jesus is Lord,' you will be saved."

The New Testament itself centers faith around **a spoken declaration**.

Divine Declaration

"Jesus is Lord."

Why These Declarations Matter

These passages reveal something important.

Faith in the Bible is not only believed in the heart; it is **spoken with the mouth**.

Declarations of faith remind us of who God is, who we are, and what promises we stand on.

When spoken sincerely, these words align our hearts with truth and strengthen our trust in God's presence and guidance.

The Seven "I Am" Words of Jesus

The Identity of Christ

In the Gospel of John, Jesus made several profound statements beginning with the phrase **"I am."** These declarations reveal His identity and mission.

Each statement echoes the divine name revealed to Moses when God said **"I AM WHO I AM."** These words remind believers that Jesus is the source of life, truth, and salvation.

These statements can also be used as **Power Whispers of devotion and reflection**.

1 — I Am the Bread of Life

Gospel of John 6:35

"I am the bread of life. Whoever comes to me shall never hunger."

Reflection Whisper

"Jesus is the bread of life. In Him my soul is satisfied."

2 — I Am the Light of the World

Gospel of John 8:12

"I am the light of the world. Whoever follows me will not walk in darkness."

Reflection Whisper

"Jesus is the light of the world, and His light guides my path."

3 — I Am the Door

Gospel of John 10:9

"I am the door. If anyone enters by me, he will be saved."

Reflection Whisper

"Jesus is the door that leads to life and salvation."

4 — I Am the Good Shepherd

Gospel of John 10:11

"I am the good shepherd. The good shepherd lays down his life for the sheep."

Reflection Whisper

"Jesus is my good shepherd, and He leads me with care."

5 — I Am the Resurrection and the Life

Gospel of John 11:25

"I am the resurrection and the life."

Reflection Whisper

"Jesus is the resurrection and the life, and in Him there is hope."

6 — I Am the Way, the Truth, and the Life

Gospel of John 14:6

"I am the way, and the truth, and the life."

Reflection Whisper

"Jesus is the way, the truth, and the life who guides me."

7 — I Am the True Vine

Gospel of John 15:5

"I am the vine; you are the branches."

Reflection Whisper

"Jesus is the true vine, and I remain connected to Him."

Why These Words Matter

These seven statements form a complete picture of Christ's role in the life of believers.

Jesus is:

- the **bread** that sustains
- the **light** that guides
- the **door** that saves
- the **shepherd** who protects
- the **life** that overcomes death
- the **way** that leads to truth
- the **vine** that nourishes growth

Together they remind us that faith is not built only on what we say, but on **who we follow**.

Seven Psalms of Strength

The Book of Psalms contains prayers, songs, and declarations that believers have spoken for thousands of years. Many of these verses are short, powerful, and perfectly suited to be whispered in moments of need.

These seven psalms are especially helpful when seeking strength, peace, and encouragement.

1 — The Lord Is My Light

Book of Psalms 27:1

"The Lord is my light and my salvation; whom shall I fear?"

Power Whisper

"The Lord is my light and my salvation. I will not fear."

2 — The Lord Is My Shepherd

Book of Psalms 23:1

"The Lord is my shepherd; I shall not want."

Power Whisper

"The Lord is my shepherd. I lack nothing."

3 — God Is My Refuge

Book of Psalms 46:1

"God Is our refuge and strength, a very present help in trouble."

Power Whisper

"God is my refuge and strength."

4 — The Lord Surrounds Me With Favor

Book of Psalms 5:12

"You surround the righteous with favor as with a shield."

Power Whisper

"The Lord surrounds me with favor like a shield."

5 — The Lord Watches Over Me

Book of Psalms 121:7–8

"The Lord will keep you from all harm."

Power Whisper

"The Lord watches over my life."

6 — The Lord Restores My Soul

Book of Psalms 23:3

"He restores my soul."

Power Whisper

"The Lord restores my soul."

7 — The Lord Renews My Strength

Book of Psalms 18:32

"It is God who arms me with strength."

Power Whisper

"The Lord fills me with strength."

Chapter 6

The Whisper That Starts Everything.

Gospel of Luke 17:21

"The kingdom of God is within you."

Closing Whisper idea

"The kingdom of God is within me."

The Final Whisper

You have spoken the Word. You have heard the truth.

You have planted the seeds of faith. Now remember this:

The power you have been whispering about is not far away.

It is already near.

Gospel of Luke 17:21

"The kingdom of God is within you."

The same Word you have spoken
is alive within you.

The same faith you have whispered
is growing within you.

The same peace you have declared
is already yours.

So keep whispering the Word.

Keep listening for truth.

And remember:

The kingdom of God
is within you.

The Grace Clause: What to Do When You Miss a Day

There will be a day when you forget.

Maybe you're traveling. Maybe you're sick. Maybe life simply gets in the way.

You wake up and realize you missed yesterday's practice.

And then comes the second thought:

"Should I start over?"

"Does this mean I've failed?"

"Is it too late to continue?"

This is where the Grace Clause comes in.

The All-or-Nothing Trap

Many people fall into the same pattern.

They begin a new habit with enthusiasm.

They commit fully for the first week.

Then something happens—a missed day, a busy schedule, a moment of weakness.

And suddenly, the entire effort feels ruined.

"I broke the chain. I might as well quit."

This is the all-or-nothing trap.

It is one of the most common reasons people abandon good intentions.

But the Grace Clause exists to free you from this trap.

The Rule

If you miss a day, do not restart. Do not punish yourself.

Do not tell yourself you've failed. Simply begin again the next day. That is all.

Why This Matters

Perfection is not the goal. Consistency is. Think of it like walking a path. If you stumble, you do not turn around and walk back to the beginning. You simply stand up and keep walking. The path does not disappear because you stumbled.

The destination remains the same.

A Biblical Perspective

The Bible speaks often about falling and rising again.

King David, after committing serious sins, wrote:

"Create in me a clean heart, O God."

He did not abandon his faith. He returned.

Peter denied Jesus three times. Yet he became a pillar of the early church. He did not let his failure define him.

He let grace restore him.

Practical Steps

If you miss a day, here is what to do:

1. Acknowledge Without Judgment

Say to yourself: *"I missed a day. That is okay."*

Do not add shame to the mistake.

2. Return Immediately

Do not wait for Monday. Do not wait for a fresh start.

Begin again today.

3. Adjust If Needed

If you're missing days regularly, the routine may need adjustment.

Try a shorter practice.

Try a different time of day.

Find what works for your life.

4. Keep the Streak Visible

If you're tracking on a calendar, leave the blank space.

Do not erase it.

Do not pretend it didn't happen.

Simply mark the next day and continue.

The Real Measure

The measure of your commitment is not whether you miss a day.

The measure is whether you return.

One missed day does not undo weeks of progress.

One missed day does not erase the seeds you've planted.

The Word you spoke still lives in your heart.

The faith you declared still shapes your thinking.

The practice still matters.

A Gentle Reminder

You are not building a perfect record.

You are building a habit. Habits are messy. They are interrupted. They are restarted. They are human.

The Promise

Forty days from now, you will not remember every single day.

You will not remember every whisper.

But you will remember how you felt.

You will remember the shift in your thinking.

You will remember the steadiness in your faith.

And you will know that even with the missed days, the practice worked.

Because you kept going.

Grace

Grace is not just for others. Grace is for you too. Be kind to yourself. Be patient with yourself.

Keep whispering the Word. Keep returning to the practice. And remember: The journey is not about perfection. It is about persistence.

Chapter 7

Violet Fire – Power Whispers

The Violet Fire is the fire of transformation. It represents the ability to release what no longer serves you and return to a state of clarity, peace, and spiritual strength.

When you speak:
"I am a being of the violet fire. I am the purity God desires,"
you are aligning your mind and spirit with renewal.

These words help shift your thoughts, clear emotional weight, and reinforce a sense of inner cleansing and purpose. Through repetition, the mind begins to let go of negativity and embrace a higher, calmer state of being.

There is also power in speaking these words in the second person:

"You are a being of the violet fire..."
This can feel like truth being spoken over you, helping the message sink deeper and bypass resistance in the mind.

You can also speak these words for others. Direct the words toward someone you want to improve your relationship with, or someone going through a difficult time (loved ones, neighbor, boss):
"First Name Last Name is a being of the violet fire. First Name Last Name is the purity God desires."
This becomes an act of intention, compassion, and blessing—shifting not only how you see them, but how you show up toward them.

This is not just imagination—it is intention in motion. Spoken daily, it becomes a practice of releasing, restoring, and returning to your true self.

Power Whisper

I am a being of the violet fire.

I am the purity God desires.

Repeat 3 times

OR

I am a being of the violet fire.

I am the purity God desires.

You are a being of the violet fire.

You are the purity God desires.

Repeat 3 times

OR

Your first name your last name is a being of the violet fire.

Your first name your last name is the purity God desires.

Repeat 3 times

Violet Fire Power Whisper for others

Their first name their last name is a being of the violet fire.

Their first name their last name is the purity God desires.

Repeat 3 times

Here is another version

Power Whisper

I am a being of the violet light.

I am the purity of Gods delight.

Repeat 3 times

OR

I am a being of the violet light.

I am the purity of Gods delight.

You are a being of the violet light

You are the purity of Gods delight.

Repeat 3 times

OR

Your first name your last name is a being of the violet light.

Your first name your last name is the purity of Gods delight.

Repeat 3 times

Violet Light Power Whisper for others

Their first name their last name is a being of the violet light.

Their first name their last name is the purity of Gods delight.

Repeat 3 times

Closing Thought

There will be days when the morning practice feels impossible.

There will be moments when you forget to breathe, let alone whisper.

On those days, remember this:

Even one word spoken in faith carries power.

Even one whisper in the darkness is heard.

Keep speaking.

Keep trusting.

Appendix A

Crisis Triggers: Power Whispers for Difficult Moments

Life does not always unfold according to plan.

There are moments when the morning routine feels too far away. When anxiety strikes in the middle of a meeting. When grief arrives at midnight. When financial stress tightens its grip.

In these moments, you need more than a scheduled practice.

You need a lifeline.

The following whispers are designed for specific crisis moments. Keep this list accessible—on your phone, in your wallet, or posted where you can see it.

When the storm hits, you won't have time to search for the right words.

These are already chosen for you.

Before a Difficult Conversation

Trigger: Meeting with someone challenging, delivering hard news, or navigating conflict

Power Whisper: "The Lord is my helper; I will not be afraid." Epistle to the Hebrews 13:6

Power Whisper: "The Lord directs my steps." Book of Proverbs 16:9

Power Whisper: "Love is patient and kind in me." First Epistle to the Corinthians 13:4

Why These Work: These verses anchor you in courage, guidance, and patience. They remind you that you are not alone in the conversation, and that wisdom is available to you.

When Anxiety Spikes

Trigger: Racing thoughts, panic, overwhelming worry

Power Whisper: "The peace of God guards my heart and mind." Epistle to the Philippians 4:7

Power Whisper: "God has not given me a spirit of fear, but power, love, and a sound mind." Second Epistle to Timothy 1:7

Power Whisper: "The Lord is my refuge and strength." Book of Psalms 46:1

Why These Work: Anxiety thrives on uncertainty. These declarations bring immediate clarity about where your safety lies—not in circumstances, but in God's presence.

Financial Stress

Trigger: Bills piling up, unexpected expenses, job insecurity

Power Whisper: "My God supplies all my needs." Epistle to the Philippians 4:19

Power Whisper: "The Lord is my shepherd; I lack nothing." Book of Psalms 23:1

Power Whisper: "The Lord blesses the work of my hands." Book of Deuteronomy 28:12

Why These Work: Money worries often trigger feelings of scarcity and fear. These verses reframe your perspective from lack to provision, acknowledging that you are cared for.

Health Concerns

Trigger: Diagnosis, pain, recovery, or caring for a sick loved one

Power Whisper: "The Lord restores my soul." Book of Psalms 23:3

Power Whisper: "I shall live and declare the works of the Lord." Book of Psalms 118:17

Power Whisper: "The joy of the Lord is my strength." Book of Nehemiah 8:10

Why These Work: Health struggles can shake your sense of control. These whispers anchor you in hope and remind you that your identity is not defined by illness.

Grief and Loss

Trigger: Death, breakup, major life transition

Power Whisper: "The Lord is close to the brokenhearted." Book of Psalms 34:18

Power Whisper: "The Lord comforts me in all my troubles." Second Epistle to Corinthians 1:4

Power Whisper: "I shall not die, but live." Book of Psalms 118:17

Why These Work: Grief isolates. These verses remind you that you are seen in your pain, and that life continues even through loss.

Feeling Overwhelmed

Trigger: Too much to do, burnout, exhaustion

Power Whisper: "The Lord gives rest to my soul." Gospel of Matthew 11:28

Power Whisper: "The Lord renews my strength." Book of Isaiah 40:31

Power Whisper: "The Lord is my strength and my shield." Book of Psalms 28:7

Why These Work: Burnout convinces you that you must carry everything alone. These declarations invite you to surrender the weight and receive strength.

When You Feel Alone

Trigger: Isolation, loneliness, feeling misunderstood

Power Whisper: "The Lord is with me wherever I go." Book of Joshua 1:9

Power Whisper: "I am chosen and dearly loved." Epistle to the Colossians 3:12

Power Whisper: "The Lord surrounds me with favor like a shield." Book of Psalms 5:12

Why These Work: Loneliness distorts reality. These verses correct the lie that you are abandoned, reminding you of your inherent worth and constant companionship.

Before Making a Decision

Trigger: Crossroads, uncertainty about next steps

Power Whisper: "The Lord guides me continually." Book of Isaiah 58:11

Power Whisper: "The Lord directs my steps." Book of Proverbs 16:9

Power Whisper: "The plans God has for me are good." Book of Jeremiah 29:11

Why These Work: Decision fatigue clouds judgment. These whispers restore trust in the process and in the One who holds your future.

A Note on Timing

These whispers are not magic spells.

They are anchors.

They do not remove the storm.

They steady you within it.

Sometimes the crisis passes quickly. Sometimes it lingers.

Either way, you are not without words.

You are not without truth.

You are not without strength.

Appendix B

Questformation™ - Questing your vision into realty.

At its heart, questformation™ is the practice of using intentional questions to shape reality. It is not a technique, it is a philosophy, a worldview, a way of navigating the fabric of the universe.

Questformation™, is not just a tool for manifestation. It is a gateway to harmonic alignment, a way of tuning consciousness to the frequency of receiving. It is not about pretending to be something you're not; it is about inviting what already *wants* to become you.

Sample Questformations™ for Rewriting Core Beliefs

Here are five common limiting beliefs and their geometric harmonizers:

Limiting Belief	Questformation™
I aways fail	Why am I successful in ll that I do?
I will not be financially free	Why am I feeling prosperous now?
Money is hard to earn	Why am I open to new opportunities?
I don't feel seen.	Why an I expressing myself freely?
I'm afraid of abandonment.	Why am I feeling more and more loved?

Wear your Power Whisper.

Speak it. Wear It. Become it.

Visit: DesignsByTheFritz.Com